The Music of the Night
And Other Poems

JOYCE KEVEREN

The Music of the Night: And Other Poems
Copyright © 2024 by Joyce Keveren

ISBN: 979-8895312001 (sc)
ISBN: 979-8895312018 (e)

All rights reserved. No part of this publication may be reproduced, distributed, or transmitted in any form or by any means, including photocopying, recording, or other electronic or mechanical methods, without the prior written permission of the publisher and/or the author, except in the case of brief quotations embodied in critical reviews and other noncommercial uses permitted by copyright law.

The views expressed in this book are solely those of the author and do not necessarily reflect the views of the publisher, and the publisher hereby disclaims any responsibility for them.

Writers' Branding
(877) 608-6550
www.writersbranding.com
media@writersbranding.com

Contents

SECTION ONE
LOVE AND OTHER IDEAS

The Music Of The Night 3
Soul Deep 4
Those Eyes 6
For Leon My Wild Lakota Child 7
Our Spirit Horses For Leon 9
Love Is A Yearning 10
Fire 11
The Stranger 12
Plans 13
Space And Time 15
Love Story 16
My Red Tail Hawk 18
Because 19
The Rain 20
Remembering 21
Desert Spring 23
Speak To Me 25

There Are Days 26
Soul Link 27
Love Lives On 28
The Favelas 30
The Power Of The Music 31
The Baseball Player And The Movie Star 33
The Love Within 34
Sea Bird 35
The Old Ones 37
For The World Suggestion Box 38

SECTION TWO
STATE OF THE UNION

There Is Help 41
Listen And Say Yes 43
Derailing 45
The Junkie's Lament 47
Walk Humbly 51
Life Span 52
Rain In The Desert 53
Overturn Those Tables 54
Some Advice 56
It's Up To You 57
Cosmic Correction 58
Just One Rule 59
The Treasure Within 60
A Teaching 61

Location Location Location 63
The Maze 65
Climate Change 67
Explosions 68
Assassination Blues 69
The Chinook Wind 71
My Teacher's Words 73
One Person 74
Red Eyes 76
An Observation From My Own Personal Hell: 78

SECTION THREE
WORLD OF WOMEN

Goodbye 80
The Battered Woman's Song 81
Sorrow 82
I Surrender 83
Paths 85
Problems 86
Mourning 87
Home 88
Regret 89
The Wild Ones 90
Wounds 91
Learning 92
The Film Noir World 93
The Silence 94

The Ball Is In Your Court 95

The Truth 96

Time 97

The Path 99

In The Light 100

The Last Rodeo 101

Moon Message 102

Genesis Update 103

SECTION FOUR
SONNETS

Sonnet #19 106

Sonnet #20 107

SECTION FIVE
SHORT BUT NOT TOO SWEET

Stop Think 110

The Destination 111

2023 Requiem 112

Yes, It's Better 113

The Fascist Wind 114

Pearls Before Swine 115

The Immigrants 116

The Great I Am 117

Sound 118

What?? 119

To Whom It May Concern 120
No More Preaching 121
A Juggler Too 122
Perhaps It's You 123
Memories 124
The Good Christian Woman 125
A Question 126
Food For Thought 127
The Darkness 128
To The Haters 129
The Old Hound Dog 130
Bleeding 131
Curiousity 132
Rock Hard 133
Envy 134
The World Isn't Ready For Mind Reading 135
The Other Side 136
She Was You 137
Waking Up 138
Negativity Squared 139

SECTION SIX
HAIKU AND SENRYU

Really?? 143
To The White Christian Nationalist 143
Nature 143
Vision 144

OMG 144
You Have One Job 144
Like The Platypus? 145
Oh-Oh 145
Advice 145
India 146
Christianity 146
Precious Metals 146
The Beasts 147
Like The Birds 147
Semantics 147
Tell Me 148
Keep Moving 148
The Moment 148
Or Damned 149
My Prayer 149
To Whom It May Concern 149
The Traveler 150
—Jesus Said— 150
Sowing And Reaping 150
Guess Who? 151
What's In A Name 151
Returns 151
The Good Old Days 152
More Good Old Days 152
Yesterday? (And Now) 152
Truth 153
Yet Another Delusion 153
The Inner War 153

Names	154
The Teachings	154
Fascist Daddy	154
One Fall Day	155
The Battered Woman	155
He Started It	155
Love	156
I Tried	156
Yesterday	156
War	157
Congratulations	157
The Fool 1	157
The Fool 2	158
You	158
The Knowitalls	158
The Protection Racket	159
Women	159
New Year	159
Right Here	160
The Despot	160
Sticks And Stones	160
Dreams	161
Victims	161
Winter	161
Alone	162
Winter Wind	162
Evangelical Stuff	162
The Sons Of Bitches	163
OMG	163

Sundown	163
Winter	164
Winter	164
Rain	164
2023	165
Do Not Enter	165
The Pearl	165
Wisdom	166
TiMe	166
To My Child	166
Saints And Sinners	167
The River Road	167
Hope	167
To My Adopted Grandchild	168
Grandma	168
Advice	168
Hindsight	169
A Message From Grandma	169
The Question	169
The Answer	170
Memories	170
Truth	170
Truth	171
Comedians	171
Hooray!	171
Gaza 2024	172
To The Women	172
Theology	172
Questions	173

We Are Light	173
21ST Century Doorman	173
A Weird Truth	174
Another Weird Truth	174
Life	174
Her Love	175
The Jury Is Still Out	175
For Dick	175
The Path	176
Baby Leaves	176
Wasted Time	176
Borders	177
21St Century	177
Memory	177
Prophicies	178
Sleep	178
Travel Plans	178
To Whom It May Concern	179
Love Your Neighbor	179
Baby Birds	179
Fools Fooling Fools	180
The Movie Star	180
The Fool	180
Defense	181
Gaza 2024	181
April	181
Lilacs	182
The Beast	182
Tears I	182

Tears II	183
You Get What You Give	183
Hearts	183
Love One Another	184
Listen, People	184
Dali's Clocks	184
AI	185
Home	185
Life After Life	185
Dawn Song	186
Many Things	186
Here And Now	186
Advice	187
Babylon	187
Paradox	187
To A Pleasure Seeker	188
Am I Dreaming	188
Requiem For O.J.	188
The Hoarder	189
Movie Plot	189
Jesus Wept	189
Life	190
For A Man	190
You	190
For You	191
All I Want	191
The Children	191
Not Just For Little Girls	192
Lilacs	192

For You	192
The Stream	193
Please	193
The Welsh	193
The People	194
The Bully	194
For Me	194
The Well	195
Strong Man??	195
Joy	195
Prayer	196
As John Lennon Said	196
A Question	196
A Grand Illusion?	197
English	197
Economics 101	197
Love And Time	198
Theology 101	198
Wild Oats	198
The Light	199
As The Beatles Said	199
Magic	199
Change	200
The Doomsday Clock	200
Star Signs?	200
Let Go	201
???	201
Selfishness	201
On Death	202

Marriage	202
Love	202
Autumn Leaf	203
Aging	203
Love	203

SECTION ONE
LOVE AND OTHER IDEAS

THE MUSIC OF THE NIGHT

I wake at midnight
to hear the birds
outside my window
jammin' like the Wailers
on a warm night
in Jamaica
when the spliffs
are burning freely
and the breeze is
whispering love.
Hush, can you hear it
singing of your longing?
Do not be afraid—
there is hope upon that wind
and a reason to be joyful,
so rejoice, my friend.

SOUL DEEP

A ring is just a ring
you can take it off
and lay it down,
it's not something
you must keep.
Vows can be broken
Just as easy
as they're said,
words are just words
vows are not something
that you have to keep.
Affairs of the heart
can end with a sigh
as you begin to weep
with your losses
and your pain.

Love will last
through storms
and betrayals
life after life
death after death
only if it
goes soul deep.

THOSE EYES

I love those dark Mediterranean eyes
those eyes from Eastern Europe
at the edge of Asia
those heavy-lidded lovely eyes
that you know take an effort
just to open—just to look at you,
those Omar Sharif--Dr. Zhivago eyes
deep and dark and filled
with love and light--yes
I love those eyes.

FOR LEON
MY WILD LAKOTA CHILD

Wild things grow
On the northern plains
Sunflowers—
Wild roses
The little white Star of Bethlehem,
Flower of the spring,
Indian paintbrush
Sweetgrass and goldenrod
Gramma grass and buffalo grass
Sagebrush and pine
Cottonwood and cactus
And so much more—

Sage chickens and grouse
Prairie dogs and pronghorn
Mule deer
White tail deer
Coyotes and wolves
Eagles and hawks

Robins and crows

Jackrabbits and rattlesnakes

Bull-snakes and bison

Gophers and muskrats

Porcupines and prairie dogs

And yes, there is more,

One more

The wildest one of all,

The best one, the sweet one,

The best loved of all—

My wild Lakota child.

OUR SPIRIT HORSES
FOR LEON

Ride your spirit horse
to the edges of the galaxy
sing your morning
song to the wind
send a message back to me
on the wings of my hawk
build a fire of starlight
to guide my horse's way
soon I will ride
with you again.

LOVE IS A YEARNING

Love is a yearning
so sharp and so deep
it is pain that goes
to the edge of your being
when you wake
and when you sleep.

Love is a burning
yellow, white and blue hot
that tears and sears
a longing that goes
beyond your knowing
feeding your sorrow
feeding your tears.

Love is a learning
of lessons so deep
and lessons so old
they awaken your soul.

FIRE

The embers from our fire
Rise into the sky
To disappear among
The stars who are
Their brothers.

THE STRANGER

The stranger at your gate
may be an old remembered friend
come home again.

PLANS

The beaches of Rio
The Champs Elysee
Ayers Rock in the Outback
The Appian Way
The Rock of Gibraltar
Victoria Falls
Machu Picchu
The Great Wall of China
Niagara Falls—
We never went there
When we were young
And the world was
Made of crystals
Gleaming under the sun
When we were in love--
No, we never went there—

So let's make a plan
To go there
In the next life-
I'll meet you in Ipanema
Whenever you can.

SPACE AND TIME

The time/space continuum
does not apply to us—
though we're apart
we are together
though time has stopped
where you are
and it goes on here
where I am--
still we are together.

LOVE STORY

She fell in love
with the skinny white boy
who played his old
Stratocaster down
on the south side
in that bar by
the railroad tracks.

Her mama told her,
when you get older
you will understand
why this will not work—
he will always be broke
and you will be hungry--
all your dreams will
go up in smoke.
You can't live on
those love songs he writes,
get a man with a job
and a haircut--

you will live a life of regret
for this white boy and his songs.

So she left him
and went back to school
and the skinny white boy
wrote love songs of loss,
got a band together,
went on the road
toured the world
got rich and famous
but never forgot
that first love he lost.
She understood
that her mother was right--
she led a life of regret
for the loss of that
skinny white boy
she could not forget.

MY RED TAIL HAWK

My red tail hawk came home
for the winter-
he flew over the house
turned south
and disappeared
into the sunlight.
It will be a good winter.

BECAUSE

Because this house
has been our shelter--
because an angel
guards the door
because this space
has witnessed loving
because we know
what love is for
I declare this house
A sacred place
where love will stay
Forevermore.

THE RAIN

Wherever I go
when I leave this earth
I want to remember the rain.
I want to remember the rain
 on the desert—
liquid life, liquid peace
liquid love.
I want to remember the rain
on the high plains
and the mountains
and on the seashore—
I want to remember
the rain that we walked in
that summer day on campus
holding hands
with heads high, laughing—
I want to remember the rain.

REMEMBERING

The moment of the loving
contained the knowing
of the end—
and yet—
the joy
and the pain
were one and
the same.
If everything is gone
And they have taken
all I have—
still I will remember
the color of your eyes
the texture of your hair
the sound of your voice
too sweet for my ear-

I did not know
till now
how little
it would take
to make me happy.

DESERT SPRING

I can feel that
spring is coming
after all the winter rain
listen—I can hear
the plants growing
in the warming earth.

The eggs in the nests
of the birds
in the mesquite
are trembling,
ready for the
baby's birth.

My red tail hawk will soon
fly over—dip his wings
in goodbye as he heads north
for his summer home.
I watch him until
he's out of sight.

The sun is
staying longer
and he's also heading north--
the flowering tree will
 blossom soon
in wild bursts of white.

I love the desert spring
where life is so determined
to show it's splendor
and it's hard-won return
in red and yellow desert daisies
and the plum tree's red and white.

I feel the same renewal
somewhere deep within,
so I put on bright colors
like the plants
and life begins again.

SPEAK TO ME

Speak to me of love—
I do not need to
understand the words—
I only need to feel
them on my skin
and let the tenderness
and joy softly seep
into my waiting soul.

THERE ARE DAYS

There are days when I think
my love has all dried up--
then I meet someone new—
someone a lot like you,
whose stories are like mine
and we share a glass of wine
and cry our flood of tears
and share all our shameful fears,
someone a lot like me
who has lost so very much
and kept on living, never giving up
and my love is new again.

SOUL LINK

We were torn from
each other's arms
by forces we could
not control—
our bodies were lost—
not together--
but they could not
control our souls.

LOVE LIVES ON

The passion--
the sex--
all that is gone,
but the love—
that love lives on.

I had been told that
love is all that will last—
and I believed it
but I did not really know
until I lived it—
got lost in it—
like an addiction,
an obsession—
I needed that fix.

And then it ended—
betrayal will do that to you,
but the love lived on
and on
and on and on
until I not only
believed it but
I knew it was true.

THE FAVELAS

The favelas of Rio
perched on the mountain
like a flock of
bright colored birds, resting,
dreaming of nesting
are beautiful, wonderful
handmade works of art—
a reflection
of the soul
of the people.
They are lovely
like the people
and I love them.

THE POWER OF THE MUSIC

Any time I listen to
Nessum Dorma done
by almost anyone,
I stop breathing
at that moment
when the music rises
and my breath changes
in some mysterious way—
the beauty of those notes
changes me all over.

November Rain, All I Ask,
and Labrinth's Jealous
can always make me cry
for all things lost
and all star-crossed
lovers everywhere
longing for a love
that's gone.

Then Marley's Is This Love
makes me believe
in love and Jah again.

The music of Thin Lizzy
makes me want to dance.
Music can move the body
and the soul.
It can soothe a broken heart
or tear you apart,
start a revolution,
give you hope
and bring you home.

THE BASEBALL PLAYER AND THE MOVIE STAR

Joltin' Joe DiMaggio
married Marilyn Monroe
and then, of course,
they got a divorce—
for that's the American way
and when she died
he surely cried,
for he had roses placed
upon her grave
almost until the day he died.

THE LOVE WITHIN

The love that
has been
within me
before the day
that I was born
has finally found
a home—
It is anywhere
that my feet
may take me
and anything
my eyes
light on.

SEA BIRD

The sea bird calls me
for that is my name
the name given me
by those children
that I loved.

I can hear it
on the wind
from the sea-
that name
given me
by those children
who loved me,
those children
I thought I had lost,
those children who
loved so easily.

They are here
with me still
still loving me
still calling me
by my name,
Seabird,
telling me that
when there is love,
nothing is ever lost.

THE OLD ONES

I share

these paths I walk--

the footsteps of the old ones

linger there

and everywhere

I look are gifts

they have left me-

I am their unnamed heir.

FOR THE WORLD SUGGESTION BOX
(the WSB)

It is illegal for me to kill someone. It is illegal for anyone and everyone to kill someone. So logically, it should be illegal for a government, which is a group of people, to kill someone. Therefore, war should be illegal.

That is logic. That is simple. That is common sense. That is true. Let's do it. Now. Let's make war illegal.

SECTION TWO
STATE OF THE UNION

THERE IS HELP

When you are troubled
and you're near the sea
take your troubles down to her
she will carry them away.

If you are not near the sea,
tell your troubles to the moon;
she and the sea are
old companions-
the moon will tell the sea
and she will carry them away.

If the moon is out of sight
on her path beyond
the far horizon,
put your bare feet
on the earth
and she will ease your pain.

There is always help,
above, beyond and below—
there is always help.

LISTEN AND SAY YES

Say yes to the birds
who sing their life story,
say yes to the blowing wind,
say yes to the lovers
who leave their love stories
on the ever-changing wind.

Say yes to the flow
of the seasons
and snow falling
on mountain tops,
say yes to the words
of the children
whose peace plan
is taking the world out
for ice cream
and planting flowers
by the path where you walk.

Listen to the birds
and the wind
and the snow
and the lovers
and the children,
always
listen to
the children
and say yes.

DERAILING

Like a train on a track
your brain follows old
remembered paths
laid down by someone
in the distant past.
Maybe they told you
God had decreed it,
maybe they told you
you really need it,
maybe they told you
it's tradition, my son,
it's an unwritten law
or it was the fashion,
your daddy and grandad
did it before you
so we implore you
to keep it alive.

But maybe, just maybe
you need to derail it
and find a new path
that is your own.

THE JUNKIE'S LAMENT

I ran out of cocaine
lost my apartment, my job and my car
and all that remained
was the addiction—
that demanding affliction
that I could not contain.
My mind did contortions
Of self-justifications,
Self-pity, anger and blame,
alleys, shelters and cold
were all that I had to my name
except for the addiction
and those hard darts of shame—
and still, I love cocaine.
I got off the cocaine
when I had to explain
to my dealer that I couldn't pay—
maybe next week, but not today-
no credit, no coke, no pay
is all that he would say.

When my small stash of hash was gone,
It wasn't too long
before I stole oxy from Dad
and though I knew it was bad
I liked the calm that it gave
which I had never had.

I got off the mushrooms
because my dealer died—
the first day I cried
the next two I tried
to find more mushrooms
and the fourth day I stayed in bed
and I thought and I read
an old Hindu text that said
meditate, my child and learn
who you really are—
then I noticed the colors
were all still there—

no mushrooms, but the
mushroom colors were still there.

Do you think this might work?
Or is it just a quirk?
Could sitting like Gandhi
In a kind of a trance
get me off these drugs?
Is there a chance?
Could life be better
if I was drug free?
The shrinks and the counselors,
Mom and Dad, everyone I
ever knew say yes, it could be,
but it's all up to me.
Oh, no, oh no, not me,
I have never been able
to depend on me.

Have you met me?
Oh, God and all the angels,
Oprah and that preacher
with the planes and the
smiles that all look fake—
maybe even the Pope,
whoever's out there,
I need help!!
Please give me some hope
So I can get off the dope—
Maybe.

WALK HUMBLY

Walk humbly on the earth,
she does not
belong to you.

She will share
everything she has
with you
to ensure that
you will live,
but she does not
belong to you.

LIFE SPAN

Earth is halfway
through her life span
4.5 billion years
another 4.5 to go—
there is something
you should know:
other worlds are being born
there will be a place to go-
this is the way it's meant to be—
life is eternal—
and so are we.

RAIN IN THE DESERT

The thunder and the wind
announce the coming
of the rain—
we desert people
lift our heads
we dance and
we rejoice—
in the desert,
rain is sacred,
rare and honey-sweet;
when the falling rain
and the thirsty
earth finally meet,
all things are sanctified and sing
with just one voice.

OVERTURN THOSE TABLES

I was happy being poor
although I know what money's for,
but it won't open the door
to heaven.
Heaven's always free
you don't need a key
just ask any tree
or any river
as it wanders
to the sea.
Ask anyone on
the Hajj to Mecca,
ask any clever woman
of the Aborigines,
ask a shaman
from Central Asia
or any lovers
that you see.

Ask that pilgrim
on his way to Galilee—
heaven's always free.
Or it should be.

SOME ADVICE

Oh, you self-righteous
hypocrites and miscreants
(I was going to say
motherfuckers, but thought
it might not be acceptable to some,)
who clutter up our lives
with your laws
and your edicts
from your halls
of congress
or the pulpits
of the land—
you need to do
some housecleaning of your own
before you tell me what to do.

IT'S UP TO YOU

Life should not be frivolous;
every moment, every hour
should be imbued with meaning.

COSMIC CORRECTION

I have heard it said
that our bodies have a soul.
That is not correct.
That is backward.
Our souls have a body,
and when our souls
leave our bodies,
life will still go on.

JUST ONE RULE

If humanity
developed accidentally
and there is no
grand design
in the mind
of someone's god,
but only just
this one life
with all its pain
and misery
and strife,
still we must be kind.

THE TREASURE WITHIN

There is treasure
without measure
deep within us.
You must dig deep
as into a diamond mine
until you find
it there for the taking
and it will
set you free.

A TEACHING

Some Pueblo Indians
taught me this
both in word
and action:

When someone comes
to see you—
give them something.

When you visit
someone's home
give them something.

If you have nothing
tangible or even if you do,
give them a story
or a song,
give them your joy,

give them your peace,
give them
your acceptance
and your love.

LOCATION LOCATION LOCATION

Astronomers tell us:
we live at the edge
of a galaxy someone
named the Milky Way.
I have seen no proof of this,
but I believe it.
It's a good story,
but if we are in it,
why don't we see we're in it?
Oh, because it's a long way away;
those stars are far away.
Okay,
so it's a long way
between the stars
that make up our constellations.
If we were at a different
place other than Earth,

those constellations
or star patterns
would, of course, be different.
It's all just like
the realtors say:
Location, location location.

THE MAZE

This life is a maze
in which I am lost;
ahead is just more
of the same
in an endless game
that I do not know
the rules of.
The wise people
all tell me
the only rule is love
and up around the bend
there is more and ever more—
so that it will never end
and the name of
this forever game
is Life in Eternity,

so what am I to do

but keep searching

here for you

in this Lost and Found Room planet

in a galaxy somewhere

in the maze?.

CLIMATE CHANGE

Winter held us hostage
in its icy arms
until spring
paid the ransom
with new life
bursting, blooming
everywhere
the floods and fire
could not reach.

Summer lay a heavy heat
on the cities and the fields
until the autumn winds
and rains broke the fever
and it all began again.

EXPLOSIONS

I hear the drums of war
on the far horizon—
mushroom clouds
bloom red and blue
and yellow white
in the night
and screams bounce
off the wind.

Oh, what will happen to us
and our fine blue world?

Well, you know,
you've heard it said—
boys will be boys
and you know,
they like to blow things up.

ASSASSINATION BLUES

I got the blues
the assassination blues
this is a situation
I did not choose
these assassination blues

Did you ever really look at
that word—assassination?
Select it, inspect it, bisect it.
dissect it, maybe reject it,
and you will see—
ASS ASS IN NATION—
you have to share an N--
Is this an accident-
two asses, in nation?
Is psoriasis an accident?
No, it's an eyesore—
words are all made up by people.

I got the assassination blues
there is a lot to lose
and it seems to me
I can't even trust
my language
and that's one more
thing to lose.
Oh yeah, that's the
assassination blues.

THE CHINOOK WIND

In a brutal February
with days of bitter below
zero cold after heavy snow,
a lovely wind
began to blow
straight as the
flight of the crow
down off the
western slopes
of the Big Horns
onto the plain below,
melting the heavy
drifts of snow.
The little frozen creek
began to flow
through the hayfield
under the warming sun
as the chinook wind,

the snow eater wind
came off the mountains
to the west,
warming the people
and the land
and for a moment
in that winter
of cold and snow,
we were blessed
by that lovely Chinook
snow eater wind.

MY TEACHER'S WORDS

My teacher said,
"Place yourself
above no one;
place yourself
below no one.
This is humility."

ONE PERSON

The next time
you fail to speak up against
an atrocity or injustice
or you fail to speak up for
kindness and love,
and you say, "What can
one person do?"
consider all these
ONE PERSONS and
what they could and did do:

Atilla the Hun
Genghis Khan
Alexander the Great
Hitler
Stalin
Putin
and in a lighter, kinder vein,
Thomas Edison
Muhammad Ali

Martin Luther King
John Lennon
John Lewis
Mother Teresa
Princess Diana
Jesus
Nelson Mandela
and so many others,
make your own list,
then think again and tell me,
what can one person do?

RED EYES

Red eyes glowing
in the dark
the rats are back!
Oh no!
Red eyes glowing
like landing lights
on a crashing plane.
Now that I'm a Buddhist,
well, a pseudo-Buddhist
searching for nirvana.
Not Cobain's Nirvana-
I cannot, must not
kill anything, not even
a goddamn rat
and I want to do things right,
so I'll just get a trap
and catch the
little bastards
and relocate them
like in Witness Protection

to an alley
or a city dump.
The Buddha was right
about everything,
there is no doubt about that,
but if these fucking rats
come back one more time,
I will HAVE to kill them
and reap my karma
when it comes.

AN OBSERVATION FROM MY OWN PERSONAL HELL:

Even if we are the only self-aware species, and that is still largely unproven, we are, and there is no doubt about this, except for the Buddha, Jesus and a few others, too dumb to know what to do with it.

SECTION THREE
WORLD OF WOMEN

GOODBYE

I have crossed the raging river
into the promised land,
a place of milk and honey
where I won't need a man.
There is no way you can fix it
I am through with you.
In this place I have dominion-
I'm no longer owned by you,
your rules do not apply here.
Go in peace, but quickly go
I have no more to say to you
Except goodbye and go.

THE BATTERED WOMAN'S SONG

She's all curled up
in the fetal position
waiting for death to come,
singing a song
about her condition
and perhaps retribution
for everything that went wrong, while
she thinks, if he calls me a whore
just one time more
or reminds me that I am dumb,
oh, so help me, help me now,
you better kill me tonight
if you want to save
your worthless life,
because I may get a knife
and end your sorry life,
perhaps even later tonight.

SORROW

The nights are long
in this winter of my sorrow
as I lay awake
waiting for tomorrow.
The children I have lost
are nearly grown;
my heart lies heavy in me
like a stone.
I see a photo of
the young one
and I know that he
that child I love
will not remember me.

I SURRENDER

I surrender
my hands are
in the air,
my weapons are
abandoned
here in the twilight
on this blood-splattered
battlefield
of wasted years
and empty dreams,
wasted tears
and ever-present
stalking fears.

I surrender,
but I know
as with everything else
I gave and gave up,
It will not be enough

for you or your hungry
angry ego.
Still—I surrender.
There is nothing else
left to do.

PATHS

The river takes the
path of least resistance
on its way back
to the sea—

But you—

You took the long way
and the hard way
so you never
made it
back to me.

PROBLEMS

I see some problems
with boob and butt implants:
1. That's a foreign substance
    you're putting in your body.
2. It takes SURGERY to
    put that foreign substance
    in your body.
3. Gravity is still there working,
    pulling everything back south.
You don't need this.
You are beautiful just
the way you are.

MOURNING

Let me mourn
just this one day
for the child
that once was—
that child who
was so brutally
mistreated by a
beast unfit
to live with wolves.

HOME

This is a land
of milk and honey
where flowers bloom
all year long
and the sun shines
almost every day
to drive the blues away.
I think I'll make
my home here
and never go away.

REGRET

All the signs were right
all the omens had come true
a double rainbow
bright as neon
close enough to touch
arched over the mountain
to the east
after the rain
that cooled the land—
you offered me your love
you offered me your hand
and I still don't understand
why I turned away—
Was it fear?
or was I still in love
with someone who was gone?

It's true, oh goddamn it's true—
the things we regret the most
are the things we didn't do.

THE WILD ONES

When all the wildness
of the heart and soul
are tethered and hobbled
and under control,
what then will we become?

When we are tamed
and our thoughts are
no longer allowed
to run free—
when fear is our master
what then will we be?

Rise up, rise up
do not pretend to love
your captor or
your captivity—
rise up, rise up,
tell the man
that you must be free.

WOUNDS

When I first got the wounds
I hid them deep within
from fear and from shame.

And then—
when I rid myself
of the source of the pain
and life was no longer
about loss and gain—
I did not need either
to hide or display them-
now I am free.

LEARNING

When I began
to understand
that the source
of the joy
and the source
of the pain
were one
and the same,
I began to lose
the fear.

THE FILM NOIR WORLD

Come—be with me now
before the day turns into night
and the bombs start exploding
into red and orange and yellow-white
bursts of light
that fill the night
with terror and this evil light
before it fades to black
in this film noir world
of our own making.

Come, be with me now,
not because of fear
but because of love
for only love
can tame
this insatiable need
for death
and destruction
that rules our black noir world.

THE SILENCE

Go into the silence
that is deep within you
away from all the chatter
and the clatter
of the world.

When your worries
are on mute
and your thoughts
are all on hold
the silence will
speak louder
than the lectures
or any sermon
ever told.

THE BALL IS IN YOUR COURT

All anyone can do
to you
is do something—
how it affects you
is up to you.

THE TRUTH

She did not like lies
or liars
so she told the truth—
her thoughts
and words
and actions
were aligned like
the three stars
in Orion's belt—
this led to inner peace
which paved the way
to happiness
where love could
make its home.

TIME

Time was a cheetah
running through the
crayon-colored days
of my childhood.
Time was a knife
cutting off all
 that I had loved,
tearing me from
the safety of
that childhood world.
Time was a predator
chasing me into
an adulthood
I was unprepared for-
Bloody, battered, raw,
I flailed around
and muddled through
paddling my leaky
old canoe

upstream against the flow

until Time finally put an end

to all the chaos

and Time became my friend

and my usher

leading me up to the end

where I can choose

a new world

where I can try again.

THE PATH

I'll take the path
along the river
when it's my
time to leave—
you do not need
to say goodbye
there is no need
to grieve.
I will see you
somewhere
in another
time and place—
and even though
it's different,
do you think
I won't know
your face?

IN THE LIGHT

Occasionally,
I look at me
and I can see
a speck of brilliance
somewhere there within
shining back at me.

And then I see
that shining light
that speck of brilliance
in everyone I see—
it's in all of us
that lovely light-
treasure it
like starlight
do not let
that light go out
nurture it
and hold it tight.

THE LAST RODEO

Yes, goddammit, this is
my first rodeo
I never loved like this before
and I never will again—
now my arms are empty
as the sun sets
beyond a wild and ragged sea.
It almost killed me,
but I had to set you free
and there will never be
another rodeo
like that for me.

MOON MESSAGE

The full moon shining
through my window
giving me the light
she stored from the
sun we share
to light up my night,
sending me her hope,
sending me her joy,
telling me that I can be
anything I choose
to work for—
telling me that bravery
is easier than fear
once you learn to use it,
telling me that life is good
and loss and sorrow
are only temporary
soon to be gone tomorrow
telling me that hope and love endure.

GENESIS UPDATE

Here is the answer to that old Genesis question, am I my brother's keeper? Yes, goddammit, you are, and your sister's too.

SECTION FOUR
SONNETS

SONNET #19

The universe cooperates with you
When you stay aware of your magic link
To Spirit whose guidance and love aid you
In what you say, how you behave and think.
Ask and it shall be given, seek and find—
Test these words, ask for something, wait and see.
If you pay attention, open your mind-
You will learn that the truth will set you free.
You have heard that you will get what you give
What you wish for others comes back to you.
You will learn there is a new way to live
Be very careful, it's coming to you.
Of course you have heard that one big rule, Love—
It applies here, there, below and above.

SONNET #20

There are so many things I want to say
About this love I've held so long for you
But time has taken some of it away
Confusing what is false and what is true
You said the man I loved was never real
That I had made him up to fill my need-
There are remnants of that love I still feel
I will not agree, I will not concede—
That deep love we had changed both you and me
The transformation was real, pure and deep
Had we stayed together, what would we be?
I see glimpses in my dreams as I sleep
Our souls will meet again, sometime somewhere
And all our questions will be answered there.

SECTION FIVE
SHORT BUT NOT TOO SWEET

STOP THINK

If you are too weak
to accept the consequences
of your actions,
you are too weak
to act.

THE DESTINATION

Fire and water
air and earth
have been
lying in wait
since the day
of your birth
to reclaim you.

2023 REQUIEM

They always say,
get the children
out of the war zone!
Don't they?
But the children
did not get out
the children did not
get out of Gaza.

YES, IT'S BETTER

Yes, we women
do have it better now—
they no longer
burn us at the stake
as witches
or throw us
into volcanos
as a sacrifice
to their male God of lust
who, they say,
is compassionate and just.

THE FASCIST WIND

The pages of history
are rustling
in the fascist wind
that is blowing
all around the world—
listen—
to the warning
in that wind.

PEARLS BEFORE SWINE

Like pearls before swine,
when you heard the truth,
you trampled it in the
mud of your ignorance
and went away
happy to be blind.

THE IMMIGRANTS

So your God is a man?
Come on, my sisters,
let's pack up and go
to a planet where
women are valued.

THE GREAT I AM

Descartes got it backward-
it is not I think
therefore I am—
it is I am
therefore I think.

SOUND

Sound brought down
the walls of Jericho-
so be careful
with your words—
they are directed sound--
they can build up
or they can tear down.

WHAT??

Go away the two of you
meander down memory lane
or wherever it is that you go—
I do not need you
not anymore—
how odd that the two of you
are both called he
and what was I, a woman
doing there, is odder yet to me.

TO WHOM IT MAY CONCERN

The imaginary trajectory of the
imaginary bullet
from my imaginary gun,
I think, an imaginary 38 special
with an imaginary
 carved ivory handle,
in my waking vision
went straight into
your imaginary forehead,
so perhaps you should go,
be quiet, and tend your garden,
leaving the rest of us,
especially me, alone.

NO MORE PREACHING

Your sure and certain
hope of heaven
may be comforting—
somehow—
but it won't solve
all these problems
I am dealing with
right now.

A JUGGLER TOO

He was a mental acrobat—
he kept his misogyny intact
while living like a parasite
off women.

PERHAPS IT'S YOU

The barbarians
at the gate—
the ones you hate
may not be
the enemy.

MEMORIES

When the pain comes

do not be afraid

for everything, even this

someday will fade

and be

just another memory.

THE GOOD CHRISTIAN WOMAN

She packed a Bible like a weapon
and told everyone who disagreed
with her warped and twisted creed
that they would soon be burning
in the everlasting fires of hell
for not heeding and not learning
all the truths she had to tell,
but don't forget, you lowly sinners
as you squirm and roast in hell,
you're still winners, yes real winners,
because her God loves you all.

A QUESTION

If the Popes are all
Infallible,
why are they always
apologizing for all
their mistakes?

FOOD FOR THOUGHT

Do not dismiss
those people
who live out there
in the margins of your
fatuous and fictional,
frivolous and fated society
run by your roly-poly
crapulous dear leader,
for among those
living there on the edges
very well may be
someone who is holy,
oh, so much more holy
than any one of you
can or ever will be.

THE DARKNESS

The darkness
that you gave me
when you left
was my enemy.

Then, as I began
to understand
that darkness became
my ally, my refuge
and my friend.

TO THE HATERS

When did you secede
from the human race
to become the face
of all that ugly hate?

THE OLD HOUND DOG

That pleading look
in your eyes
like a hungry
old hound dog
won't work anymore—
not for me—
not after this
third goddamn
woman and that
kid of hers. And yours.
You need put out
of my misery.

BLEEDING

It finally
occurred to me
that you were
just as changed
just as moved as I
just as torn apart
with each goodbye
ripped open by
the strange
and awful pain
of love so deep
it left us open wide
to bleed out all alone.

CURIOUSITY

Curiosity may have
killed the cat,
but without curiosity,
there would be
no new ideas,
no new ways
of seeing things
no new ways
of thinking and
no new ways of doing—
so fuck the cat.

ROCK HARD

A brain that is
full of anger
hatred and
thoughts of revenge
is a brain that is
either rotting
or as hard and rigid
as Stonehenge.

ENVY

Envy lies heavy
on you
dragging you down
making you small—
you want the love
that was given to me,
but no—
you must get your own.

THE WORLD ISN'T READY FOR MIND READING

ESP is hard.
When I can see people's thoughts,
it is just awful.

THE OTHER SIDE

On the other side,
when they ask you,
"Did you leave the world
better than it was when
you found it?"
What will your answer be?
If everything you thought
and said and did
was all for you and only you,
what should your answer be??

SHE WAS YOU

She was young and fresh
and on her face
there wasn't a trace
of sorrow—
all that would come
on some
far away unknown
tomorrow.

WAKING UP

Now that I am old—
oh, so very old,
I have heard the
stories of the
lucky ones
who died peacefully
in their sleep.

Oh, yeah, right, but waking up
is a wonderful gift
that I did not appreciate
when I was young.

NEGATIVITY SQUARED

For her, the ultimate
pessimist, the glass is
not just half empty,
but some asshole spit in it.

SECTION SIX
HAIKU AND SENRYU

REALLY??

White fragility??
Don't be ridiculous. It's
justification.

TO THE WHITE CHRISTIAN NATIONALIST

Obviously it's
you who are inferior—
you are filled with hate.

NATURE

If you can't see the
mind of the Creator in
nature, look again.

VISION

I live on a bluff
overlooking the river
that flows to the sea.

OMG

If AI is boss
our government will be called
a technocracy.

YOU HAVE ONE JOB

For the love of God
you have been given one job—
love one another.

LIKE THE PLATYPUS?

What if there are no
post-apocalyptic times?
What if we all die?

OH-OH

"Well, this didn't work—
It's back to the drawing board,"
said God to mankind.

ADVICE

"Don't ever look back,"
said Lot's wife, "or you'll wind up
in a salt shaker."

INDIA

I love India
where beggars and insane folks
are holy people.

CHRISTIANITY

What Jesus did was
so much more than they give him
any credit for.

PRECIOUS METALS

The dawn was golden
today; silver light at noon
copper at sundown.

THE BEASTS

the wolves of anger
and the beasts of discontent
are soothed by laughter.

LIKE THE BIRDS

Trembling in the wind
as the snow begins to fall,
I want to fly south.

SEMANTICS

It's all relative;
one person's matchmaking is
another's pimping.

TELL ME

How do we forgive
when the blood of the children
cries out for justice?

KEEP MOVING

When you get old, you
have to keep moving or they
just might bury you.

THE MOMENT

We all have that brief
shining moment when we are
young and beautiful.

OR DAMNED

The river of peace
that flows through the universe
should never be dammed.

MY PRAYER

When night has fallen
and there is peace in the stillness,
hear my prayer, oh Lord.

TO WHOM IT MAY CONCERN

Your misogyny
will guarantee no woman
will ever love you.

THE TRAVELER

Enslaved by glamour
beguiled by selfish desires
you wander through hell.

—JESUS SAID—

Your job is to love
whoever and whatever
is put before you.

SOWING AND REAPING

This is your karma:
The misery you dished out
has come back to you.

GUESS WHO?

There's always a turd
floating there in the punch bowl
of our happiness.

WHAT'S IN A NAME

The Sadducees and
the Pharisees are now
called Christian preachers.

RETURNS

Put that kindness you
showed me today in the bank
for a rainy day.

THE GOOD OLD DAYS

Remember when it
was accepted that men would
beat their wives and kids?

MORE GOOD OLD DAYS

Remember when it
was just accepted that priests
would molest altar boys?

YESTERDAY? (AND NOW)

Remember when it
was just accepted that WAR
would always happen?

TRUTH

It is always the
truth that makes us angry so
make your truth better.

YET ANOTHER DELUSION

I like to think that
I'm okay or better yet
that I'm wonderful.

THE INNER WAR

I try not to let
my ignorance overrule
my good common sense.

NAMES

Who thinks of these names?
Psoriasis is
truly an eyesore.

THE TEACHINGS

Don Juan told Carlos:
Another name for evil
is stupidity.

FASCIST DADDY

Household dictator
you hold the children hostage
to get what you want.

ONE FALL DAY

Three little brown birds
eating seeds in my back yard
chirping and happy.

THE BATTERED WOMAN

She was beaten down
stripped of all desire to live
yet her soul was free.

HE STARTED IT

Who fired the first shot?
Does it really matter now?
Everyone is dead.

LOVE

Love is elusive
It lies just beyond your reach
beyond your ego.

I TRIED

I tried to love you
Out of duty, out of shame—
I could not do it.

YESTERDAY

Only yesterday
we were living in darkness
dreaming of the light.

WAR

Blood of the children
cries out for an end to this:
the killing must stop.

CONGRATULATIONS

So you had a plan
To get rich or die trying—
Now you have them both.

THE FOOL 1

You poor misguided
fool—hating everything that
comes into your view.

THE FOOL 2

You pompous jackass
beating on your ego drum
and nobody cares.

YOU

You gave me your love
like rain falls from the heavens
with no strings attached.

THE KNOWITALLS

If we only knew
as much as we think we know
we would be like gods.

THE PROTECTION RACKET

When the church asks for
money, it's like extortion:
Pay or burn in hell.

WOMEN

Women all around
the world are awakening
the abuse must stop.

NEW YEAR

The new year is here—
there is noise from the fireworks--
time is seamless, still.

RIGHT HERE

My happy place is
anywhere I happen to
be at any time.

THE DESPOT

You sow chaos, hate
and pain everywhere you go—
now you want to rule?

STICKS AND STONES

There is always more
than one way to say something
there are many words.

DREAMS

When I fell in love
I allowed myself to dream
It would always be.

VICTIMS

A lot of victims
victimize themselves because
no one else wants to.

WINTER

The sunshine is weak
on this icy winter day
as I wait for spring.

ALONE

Poor sad dictator
Nobody ever loved him
He's always alone.

WINTER WIND

I want to can this
chilling wind of winter to
open in July.

EVANGELICAL STUFF

Your eternal fires
of hell do not frighten me
as much as your hate.

THE SONS OF BITCHES

Men can't even curse
each other without dragging
women into it?

OMG

The terrible twos
and all your midlife crises
look about the same.

SUNDOWN

Come sit here with me
we will watch the sun go down
on this lovely day.

WINTER

Under all that snow
the buds of spring are waiting
to be born again.

WINTER

The blossoms of spring
the white, the pink, the yellow
still color our dreams.

RAIN

A light misty ran
fell most of today on the
thirsty desert land.

2023

Women are equal
to men—please behave as though
you understand this.

DO NOT ENTER

You suck all the air
from a room when you enter—
don't enter my room.

THE PEARL

The pearl of great price
is not a real pearl but the
peace it brings is real.

WISDOM

Question everything-
the wisdom of the ages
might just be blather.

TIME

The river of time
flows in one direction—
maybe—or does it?

TO MY CHILD

Why do you doubt me?
Have I not proven my love
with my very life?

SAINTS AND SINNERS

Saints and sinners are
alike; we are all the same:
saints in the making.

THE RIVER ROAD

Take the river road
way up into the mountains
there you may find peace.

HOPE

Do not ever give up
no matter what the world brings—
there is always hope.

TO MY ADOPTED GRANDCHILD

Blood may be thicker
than water, yes, that is true
but love does not care.

GRANDMA

Featherbeds and warm
flannel sheets for winter cold—
Grandma, I miss you.

ADVICE

The way of the world
can be unkind, violent
and sad. Avoid it.

HINDSIGHT

Sometimes when I think
back on the things I have done,
I am just appalled.

A MESSAGE FROM GRANDMA

Do not give up hope—
all the lost ones will come home
when the time is right.

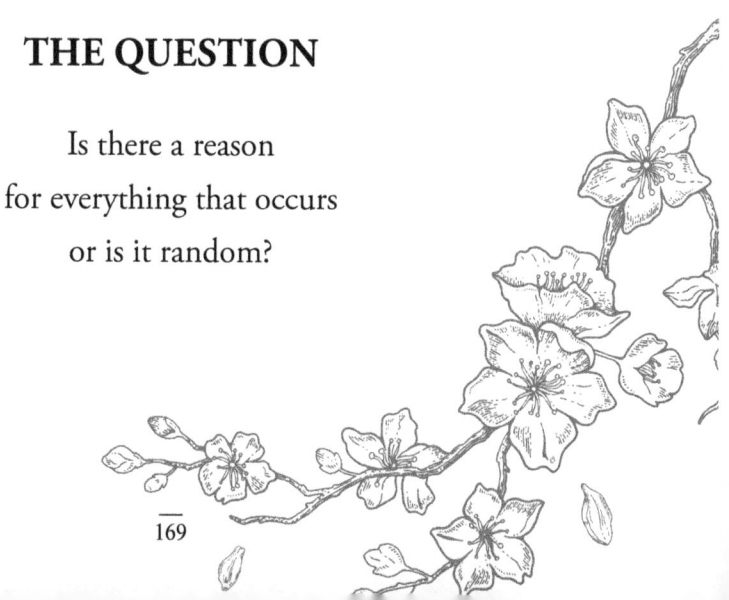

THE QUESTION

Is there a reason
for everything that occurs
or is it random?

THE ANSWER

It must be karma
because we get what we give,
so give only good.

MEMORIES

I will remember
the sweetness of your kisses
even when I'm dead.

TRUTH

Do you understand
the universal truth that
we are all equal?

TRUTH

I have witnessed this:
We all share the Great Spirit
This is a great truth.

COMEDIANS

It is often the
comedians who see things
so very clearly.

HOORAY!

It will be women
who figure out how to end
all these goddamn wars.

GAZA 2024

WTFBB??
Oh, God, you're killing children—
someone should stop you.

TO THE WOMEN

Women of the world:
Unite, stand up, rebel, sing.
Freedom will be ours.

THEOLOGY

Just because you say
that you are speaking for God
does not mean you are.

QUESTIONS

Have you lost your mind?
Voting for a dictator?
You don't like freedom?

WE ARE LIGHT

A physicist said
our bodies are all made of light
solidified light.

21ST CENTURY DOORMAN

"May I take your hat,
coat and your AR-15?
Thank you very much."

A WEIRD TRUTH

All of this stuff that
I think I know is like an
Igloo in L.A.

ANOTHER WEIRD TRUTH

Napoleon wrote
a romance novel. Say what?
That doesn't seem right.

LIFE

Life is always full
of mystery and magic-
let yourself see it.

HER LOVE

She really loved him-
her love was like a tiger
held captive too long.

THE JURY IS STILL OUT

Pandora and Eve
were both wrongly accused of
unleashing evil.

FOR DICK

Everyone loves you
All you have to do is smile
and the world is yours.

THE PATH

When you set your feet
on the Path of the Spirit,
you will not turn back.

BABY LEAVES

Newborn leaves of spring
tremble in the April wind
that will bring the rain.

WASTED TIME

Here we humans are
wasting time on hate and war
when we could be gods.

BORDERS

People who live in
border towns understand that
borders are not real.

21ST CENTURY

This situation
calls for some plain common sense—
OMG! We're out!

MEMORY

Memory can be
faulty especially if
you tell yourself lies.

PROPHICIES

There will come a time
when war will be no more and
peace will rule the land.

SLEEP

Go back to sleep, Love,
this life was just a dream
you will awake from.

TRAVEL PLANS

My soul will leave my
body and I will be free
to leave the planet.

TO WHOM IT MAY CONCERN

Your religion is
not only a crutch for you
but a weapon too.

LOVE YOUR NEIGHBOR

Jesus would say this
if he looked at all this mess:
I gave you ONE job.

BABY BIRDS

Baby birds of spring
have already learned to fly.
They're pleased with themselves.

FOOLS FOOLING FOOLS

Hiding behind words
the educated racists
only fool themselves.

THE MOVIE STAR

His jawline looked as
though it had been chiseled by
Michealangelo.

THE FOOL

You are a damn fool
if you think you are better
than anyone else.

DEFENSE

I'm too defensive
I can see that now through the
sights of this rifle.

GAZA 2024

Rivers of sorrow
flow all through the land mixing
with the children's blood.

APRIL

The palo verde blooms
with bursts of yellow light
that delights my eyes.

LILACS

Grandma's lilac bush
blooming in the northern spring
a gift from the sun.

THE BEAST

If you can look at
great suffering and not care —
then you are a beast.

TEARS I

Tears did not move you
except to make you angry
now I do not cry.

TEARS II

I stopped the tears and
became strong enough to leave
now you are crying.

YOU GET WHAT YOU GIVE

If you have been kind
there will always be someone
who is kind to you.

HEARTS

"Where your treasure is,
there will your heart be also."
If you have a heart.

LOVE ONE ANOTHER

Listen to me now
we need Marley's message
more than ever now.

LISTEN, PEOPLE

Speak only for love
Speak for redemption and peace
Peace and love will win.

DALI'S CLOCKS

Dali's clocks all melt
into the river of time—
does that mean something?

AI

I'm not a robot
Wait. Or am I? I don't know.
How can I be sure?

HOME

Oh, my childhood home—
I can go there in my dreams
and that is enough.

LIFE AFTER LIFE

I will go from life to life
to life always seeking you
and I will find you.

DAWN SONG

My birds sing at dawn
to announce the sun's return—
time to celebrate.

MANY THINGS

We are many things—
all of us—lovers, haters,
not-give-a-damners.

HERE AND NOW

Live in this moment
please do not live in the past-
it's no longer real.

ADVICE

Do not have a child
until you are ready to
love it forever.

BABYLON

Babylon will tease
with promises to please you—
all of it is lies.

PARADOX

Minimalism
Requires a lot of restraint—
less really is more.

TO A PLEASURE SEEKER

Listen to me, Boy,
do not wander into hell
as you seek pleasure.

AM I DREAMING

I am not insane,
but I have seen the sunrise
in another world.

REQUIEM FOR O.J.

You won't get away
with murder because Divine
justice waits for you.

THE HOARDER

He was a hoarder-
like a vacuum cleaner, he
sucked up everything.

MOVIE PLOT

Oh, my God, the world
is spinning off its axis
and we all will die.

JESUS WEPT

She said God is love
then spent her life hating—
that's Christianity.

LIFE

Trying something new
always experimenting—
that's what life is for.

FOR A MAN

When you understand
the power of your woman,
then you will be loved.

YOU

This is me speaking
telling of my addiction
and it's name is you.

FOR YOU

That river of tears
that follows me like a curse—
it is all for you.

ALL I WANT

All I want is peace
to give this life some meaning,
for with peace comes love.

THE CHILDREN

The dereliction
of duty applies to those
who abandon kids.

NOT JUST FOR LITTLE GIRLS

Pink is the fire and
blood of red, tempered by the
purity of white.

LILACS

I remember this:
the sweetness of the lilacs
in my Grandma's yard.

FOR YOU

I'm in love with you—
it's like a goddamn sickness
and there is no cure.

THE STREAM

Take my hand, my love
as we wade into the stream
of time together.

PLEASE

The Irish do have
a way with words, so kiss the
Blarney Stone for me.

THE WELSH

The Welsh are my folks
from my grandmother's people
I do love them so.

THE PEOPLE

Everywhere you go
you will find lovely people
made for you to love.

THE BULLY

He had a mean streak
right beside the yellow streak
that ran down his spine.

FOR ME

I can be happy
even when I'm pissed, it's just
my super power.

THE WELL

Within all of us,
there is a great well of love
draw from it daily.

STRONG MAN??

So you're a strong man?
Then why whine like a baby
every goddamn day?

JOY

Joy is in small things—
sharing your food and your time
loving your neighbor.

PRAYER

When you realize
every thought and every word
is a prayer, take care.

AS JOHN LENNON SAID

No need to outlaw
religion—just let it die
a natural death.

A QUESTION

I hear the sound of
boots on the ground in my dreams—
will they drop those bombs?

A GRAND ILLUSION?

Were you a figment
of my imagination?
Was that love not real?

ENGLISH

Isn't it odd that
the words shameless and shameful
mean the same thing?

ECONOMICS 101

This just might be true:
Inflation is one more way
to keep the poor poor.

LOVE AND TIME

Yes, we are old now,
love is not just for the young
love is for all time.

THEOLOGY 101

Creation stories
are fantasy because we
don't know anything.

WILD OATS

For men, they call it
sowing wild oats, for women,
they call it whoring.

THE LIGHT

Even the deepest
darkness of the night is filled
with the sparkling light.

AS THE BEATLES SAID

People don't need fixed—
give up trying to fix them-
all they need is love.

MAGIC

Please open your eyes—
the world is full of magic
put there for your use.

CHANGE

Change is always there.
Continents submerge and change-
nothing stays the same.

THE DOOMSDAY CLOCK

At ninety seconds
to midnight on the Doomsday
Clock, love is all we have.

STAR SIGNS?

Is our destruction
written in the stars? Must we
start over again?

LET GO

Let go gracefully
for nothing belongs to you
other than your love.

???

Question everything—
the wisdom of the ages
just might be bullshit.

SELFISHNESS

When you do not care
for anyone but yourself-
your life is empty.

ON DEATH

Let all things you do
be tempered by the knowledge
your death lies ahead.

MARRIAGE

That marriage was a
battlefield splattered with blood-
most of which was mine.

LOVE

If you are loving
you will get love, if you are
hateful, you get hate.

AUTUMN LEAF

Trembling like a leaf
in the last wind of autumn,
she clung to her love.

AGING

She was full of sighs
and tears that turned to bitter
anger as she aged.

LOVE

My teacher told me
Anything you do in love
Is always all right.